Thinking about God

Susan McCaslin

Illustrated by Dorry Clay

XXIII
TWENTY-THIRD PUBLICATIONS
Mystic, Connecticut 06355

Mommy, you know how we talk about God sometimes?

What is God?

Well, I would call God the one who makes the world, the Creator.

Mommy, did God make everything?

Yes, God is the Spirit that makes everything.

Even now God is making the world.

Then that means God is making the trees so green and tall.

God is making the sky so magic and blue.

God is making all the animals and bugs and bees and fishes, and people too.

Mommy, why does God make the bee's stinger?

Perhaps so the bee can protect itself.

Because it is very small, Mom?

Yes, because it is very small.

Mommy, can you see God?

Well, not in the ordinary way of seeing. God is more like the wind.

I get it! God is like the wind because we can't see God but God is there. I like that idea, Mom, because the wind can be very gentle and also very strong.

Mommy, why did God make the wind?

What do you think, darling?

Maybe to cool our faces when it gets too hot.
Maybe to give the birds a boost across the sky.

I think those are great ideas.

Mom, is God in the sky?

Yes, God is in the sky but also in the earth.

Is God's life in the birds, the bears, the ants, the worms?

Oh, yes, in everything, everywhere.

Mommy, is God's life in me?

Yes, God is in you all the time. God is more than you and outside of you, but God is also within you.

Mommy, I have another idea about God. I think God is what turns a seed into a beautiful flower. God is inside the seed thinking what it wants to be, and out pops a flower with a beautiful smell. Maybe the beautiful smell is God's breath.

I think that's a wonderful idea.

Mommy, I think
God loves the flowers
and the sky and the ocean
and the fish. I think God has so
much love that the love goes on and on
and never stops.

But does God love me more than you and
Daddy love me?

*God loves you as much and more, but God
loves you through us too. Our love is part of
God's love.*

But is God like a father, Mom?

Yes, God is like a father whose love goes on and on forever.

God must have strong arms then and a heart as wide
as the ocean.

Mommy, is God
like a mother?

*Yes, God is like a mother who
gives birth to a child.*

Mom, do you think no
matter where you are or
what you do, God is like a
mother who loves you?

Yes, God is
like a mother bird
with soft feathers and wide
wings who rocks you and carries
you everywhere.

Mom, sometimes you call God she and
sometimes he. Is God a man or a woman?

Well, I would say that God sometimes seems like one or the
other, but God is both, and more. God is really a great creative spirit.

Mommy, does God love everybody? Does God love
all my friends?

Yes, God loves everybody and every single one of your friends.

Does God love me and my friends and everybody else even
when we don't behave?

Yes, certainly.

Well, Mom, there's a big problem then. How can God love
pirates who steal things and make people walk the plank?

*Well, it's true that God is against stealing and harming others, so
God might not like the things pirates do, but I'm sure God still
loves them.*

Mom, I have another question. Does God laugh?

What do you think?

Well, Mom, I think God laughs whenever people are happy. I think God loves to laugh and have a good time enjoying everything.

Mom, I think God makes it sunny, but God also makes it rain sometimes for the slugs and snails. Mom, do you know why God makes it rain for the slugs?

Why dear ?

Because they like to be mushy.

Mommy, you know how we say our prayers to God at bedtime?

Yes.

Well, I think the stars pray too.

How do the stars pray?

The stars pray, Mommy, without lifting their hands. They pray by shining their light.

I think that's quite possibly true. I never saw it that way.

Mom, not all kids talk about God the way we do. I really like to think about God sometimes, and I like to talk about God with you.

I really like it, too.